FROM,

____

Mom,
it's your
day!

MEMORIES

for the
best mom

IN THE WORLD

Für die beste
MAMA
der Welt!

Mom
you are my
hero

Mom,
I love
you!

Día
de la
mamá

BEST
MOM
EVER

BEST
MOM
EVER

You are
ALWAYS
in
my heart

I love
you,
mom

Thank you Mom for All your Love

you've
got this
MAMA

My Mom
is
the best

save this
moment

MOM Happy Mother's Day!
Coloring Card

www.ingramcontent.com/pod-product-compliance
Lightning Source LLC
Chambersburg PA
CBHW051932250726